Florence, Italy: Birthplace of the Renaissance

Children's Renaissance History

BABY PROFESSOR

EDUCATION KIDS

Speedy Publishing LLC
40 E. Main St. #1156
Newark, DE 19711
www.speedypublishing.com
Copyright 2016

What has Florence, Italy
contributed to Europe
and to the world?

In this book you will learn about Florence, Italy and why it is considered as the birthplace of the Renaissance.

When was the Renaissance?

The Renaissance started at different times in different parts of Europe, but took place generally between 1300 and 1600. Europe during that time moved from the limitations of the Middle Ages toward our modern period.

What do you know about Florence, Italy?

Florence is a beautiful city. Its impressive historic architecture, magnificent monuments and striking culture have gained great admiration from all over the world.

The city was founded by Julius Caesar in 59 BC. He first named the place Florentia, which means "flourishing". He made the place as a new city for retired military veterans.

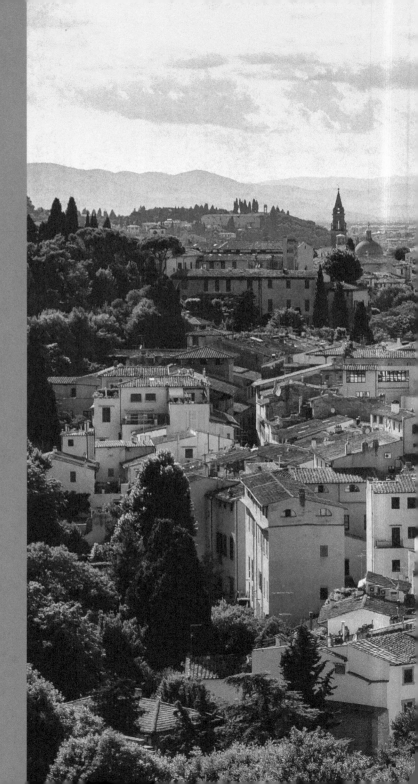

Florence is considered one of the most influential cities of Northern Italy. This breathtaking city is located in the central region of Tuscany.

Why it has become one of the most visited tourist destinations in the world?

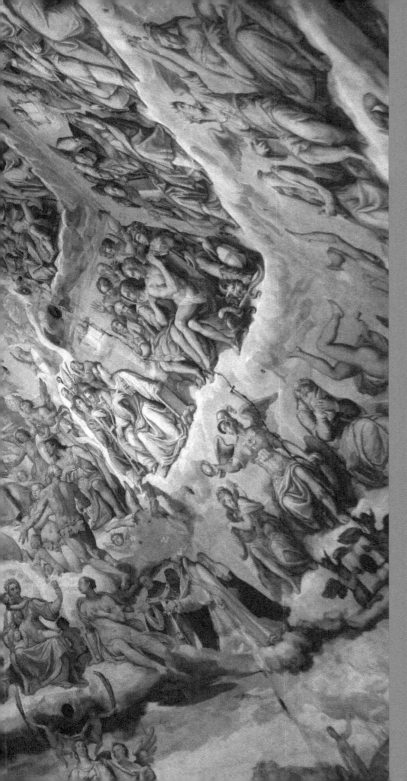

Florence is the home of great artistic treasures. The city has achieved prosperity through its arts and culture. This is why it is considered as the birthplace of the Renaissance. Florence has influenced northern Italy, all of Europe, and the whole world.

During the Middle Ages and the Renaissance, Florence was known for its arts and business achievements. Being located in rich farming land and on a major travel route between northern Italy and Rome, Florence became a great commercial centre.

The city's beautiful
buildings and
monuments
have captivated
the hearts and
admiration of
its visitors.

It became one of
the most admired
cities in Europe.

Major landmarks in the city were constructed during the Renaissance. Today, the impressive attractions of past times have become a perfect invitation to people and tourists from all over the world.

What is the Renaissance?

It is the period of great social and cultural change in Europe. It was felt across Europe from the 14th to the 16th centuries.

Renaissance means "rebirth" in French. It signifies a great revival of the classical arts and the intellect curiosity of Ancient Greece and Rome.

What was the Renaissance like? The Renaissance was a period of great art, architecture, science and philosophy which which built on and extended the achievements of the past. It is a period which is considered as the rebirth of Europe after the difficult Middle Ages.

The Renaissance was a time of great social and cultural change in Europe. Great imagination and creativity flourished. It was a great revival and renewal of Europe's classical past.

It was a great movement towards prosperity. Florence has grown towards prosperity since the 10th century.

What were the
achievements
during the
Renaissance?

New trends and styles in clothing, art, inventions, and ideas emerged during the Renaissance. Many elements of our modern culture, including our freedom to explore, to imagine, and to innovate, would not be possible without the developments of the Renaissance.

Did you enjoy reading this book? Share this to your friends.

Visit

BABY PROFESSOR
EDUCATION KIDS

www.BabyProfessorBooks.com

to download Free Baby Professor eBooks
and view our catalog of new and exciting
Children's Books